The Cutty Sark
A Kid's Guide To The Cutty Sark, Greenwich, UK

Photography by John D. Weigand
Poetry by Penelope Dyan

Bellissima Publishing, LLC
Jamul, California
www.bellissimapublishing.com

Copyright © 2014 by Penny D. Weigand and John D. Weigand

All rights reserved. No part of this book may be reproduced or transmitted in any form or by any means, electronic or mechanical, including photocopying, recording, or by any other means, or by any information or storage retrieval system, without permission from the publisher.

ISBN 978-1-61477-134-0

First Edition

"They that go down to the sea in ships, that do business in great waters, these see the works of the Lord and his wonders in the deep."

The Holy Bible, Psalms 107:23-24

"This book is for the late Julius Petersen, who as strange as it may seem, went to sea aboard a steamer ship (from Denmark) at the age of seventeen."

Penelope Dyan

The Cutty Sark
Bellissima Publishing, LLC

Introduction

The Cutty Sark is a British clipper ship. Built on the Clyde in 1869 for the Jock Willis shipping line, it was one of the very last tea clippers to be built and one of the fastest. The ship was built at the end of a long period of design development that was halted as sailing ships gave way to ships driven by steam propulsion. You see, this ship used the power of the wind and gathered the wind in its sails to further its journey, The Cutty Sark was very badly damaged by fire on May 21, 2007 as it was under restoration. It was re-opened to the public on April 25, 2012, to the delight of all would be seafaring kids and adults.

Take a look at the Cutty Sark from below and above through the lens of John D. Weigand. Practice reading skills through using word recognition, word repetition and rhyme as you learn some fun facts, and then get to work on some research of your own! The point of these books by Dyan and Weigand is to make kids not only learn, but to also help them learn to think, as well as to imagine. Award winning author, attorney and former teacher, Penelope Dyan, loves kids, loves to learn (herself) and loves it when kids learn There is a free music video that goes along with this book on YouTube on the Bellissimavideo YouTube channel to further enhance the learning process.

The Cutty Sark
Bellissima Publishing, LLC

The Cutty Sark
A Kid's Guide To The Cutty Sark, Greenwich, UK

Photography by John D. Weigand
Poetry by Penelope Dyan

With sails unfurled to the wind,
and a compass to guide the way,
the Cutty Sark rode the ocean waves,
its steady course to stay.

A fine cargo, the ship it did carry,
for every man on board and beast,
enough food and drink for its crew,
to eat for many days, a feast!
And rope and tools and many a thing,
to far away places they would bring.

And these were the finest tools
of the day,
used to help the captain and his crew,
as they sailed on their way.

Captain Woodget on board

These instruments – a speaking trumpet, a barometer and a chronometer – all belonged to Woodget, master of Cutty Sark 1885-1895.

And the captain steered steady
his course on the sea,
filled with creatures of the deep,
as strange as could be.

Here is another story I now tell,
and that is why the sailors
rang the bell.
The bell set time and watch,
and it rang throughout night and day,
as this grand old clipper ship
sailed the seas to far away.
This brass bell
was kept clean by the cook
who made sure it kept
its polished look.

You imagine sailors
in bell bottom trousers walking
right here!
You look over the side,
mom says,
"Please don't fall overboard, my dear."
And then she adds,
"It's a long, long way down, whether you
hit the water or hit the ground."
Dad tells you a story about a pirate
named Frank,
who stole some sea rations
and had to walk the plank.
You decide the story isn't true,
because he laughed as he told you.

You go into a deck cabin,
and you peek out the door.
You say,
"Come inside and see some more!"

You see the berths, the sailors' beds,
where seafaring men lay their heads.
You wonder if (in their sleep)
they dreamed dreams of oceans deep;
because you know, if this was you,
you would most certainly dream
of the ocean blue.
You would dream dreams
of mermaids all with tails,
and of giant squids and giant clams,
and of dolphins and of whales!

And you wonder if the steward
when he sat at his chair,
read that book,
and at that picture would stare,
as the ship bounced and swayed
on the sea so far from home,
and if he felt so all alone.

The pantry seems a cheery space,
every cup and saucer is set in place.
You wonder how this could ever be,
when upon a course upon the sea.
The ship would certainly sway
to and fro,
and upon the ground
those dishes would go!

The captain's table
glistens with shine,
and you decide the food
for the captain and his officers,
must have been quite fine.
You notice that a lamp is lit,
and that under the porthole
is a comfortable place to sit.

You go downstairs and look up high.
the Cutty Sark is silhouetted
against the white fogged sky.
The site of it inspires your very soul,
even if off to sea,
you would NOT like to go.
And yet, if you could travel aboard
THIS fine clipper ship,
you imagine it would be quite a trip!

Then you take one last walk.
You do some hands-on stuff,
you learn, and you talk.
Then you look up at your parents
with a big smile on your face!
You say,
"This is REALLY an amazing place!"
That night you dream,
just like me,
of traveling to far off lands
upon the sea.

"O Captain! My Captain!
Our fearful trip is done,
the ship has weathered every rock,
the prize we sought is won..."

Walt Whitman

www.ingramcontent.com/pod-product-compliance
Ingram Content Group UK Ltd.
Pitfield, Milton Keynes, MK11 3LW, UK
UKHW060136240426
12048UKWH00002B/63